The Fixer

Level 8 – Purple

Helpful Hints for Reading at Home

The graphemes (written letters) and phonemes (units of sound) used throughout this series are aligned with Letters and Sounds. This offers a consistent approach to learning whether reading at home or in the classroom. Books levelled as 'a' are an introduction to this band. Readers can advance to 'b' where graphemes are consolidated and further graphemes are introduced.

HERE IS A LIST OF ALTERNATIVE GRAPHEMES FOR THIS PHASE OF LEARNING. AN EXAMPLE OF THE PRONUNCIATION CAN BE FOUND IN BRACKETS.

Phase 5 Alternative Pronunciations of Graphemes			
a (hat, what)	e (bed, she)	i (fin, find)	o (hot, so)
u (but, unit)	c (cat, cent)	g (got, giant)	ow (cow, blow)
ie (tied, field)	ea (eat, bread)	er (farmer, herb)	ch (chin, school, chef)
y (yes, by, very)	ou (out, shoulder, could, you)		
o_e (home)	u_e (rule)		

HERE ARE SOME WORDS WHICH YOUR CHILD MAY FIND TRICKY.

Phase 5 Tricky Words			
oh	their	people	Mr
Mrs	looked	called	asked
could			

TOP TIPS FOR HELPING YOUR CHILD TO READ:

- Allow children time to break down unfamiliar words into units of sound and then encourage children to string these sounds together to create the word.

- Encourage your child to point out any focus phonics when they are used.

- Read through the book more than once to grow confidence.

- Ask simple questions about the text to assess understanding.

- Encourage children to use illustrations as prompts.

This book is a 'b' level and is a purple level 8 book band.

The Fixer

Written by John Wood

Illustrated by Amy Li

The Prime Minister was asleep when her door burst open. Her room filled with lots of people. They looked terrified.

"Wake up," they shouted in chorus.

"But it is night time. I'm tired," groaned the Prime Minister.

"No, Prime Minister. It is ten o'clock in the morning," said a small woman.
"The Sun has not come up!" said a hairy man while pointing at the window.

Their faces were white with fear. "The Sun isn't working!" screamed a tall woman.
"We are going to die!" screamed a wide man.

"Stop yelling," said the Prime Minister. She slowly stretched out her aches and let out a big yawn. Then she picked up her phone. She pressed nine numbers very carefully and said, "Hello? Is that the Fixer? We need you."

Far away in space, the Fixer got out of bed. He jumped up, hit his head on the roof and fell down the stairs. Then he had a piece of slime and goo pie for breakfast.

He fed his alien mice, which were very nice.
He put on his hat and tie. He was about to go,
but he stopped. He'd almost forgotten!

He kissed his wife. Then he went to see his sleeping children. He gently patted them on the head and smiled.

After only crashing his ship seven times, the Fixer was on his way to his first job of the day, on Earth.

The Fixer pushed a big button. Fire came out of the back of the ship, and it flew through space even faster. Then the Fixer pushed the stop button.

The Fixer was heading to Earth too quickly! He pushed the stop button again and again. It was too late. The ship crashed into the side of the Prime Minister's house.

"Ah, it is the Fixer," said the Prime Minister, wiping dust off her dressing gown. "What a relief. Our Sun isn't working. Can you help?"

"Is this the Fixer?" asked the wide man. "He doesn't even have hands!"

"He is stuck in the bin!" said the tall woman. It was true.

"He can't make the Sun rise," said the hairy man. "He is half my size!"
"His head is stuck again!" said the small woman.

"He cannot even say anything," said the wide man. The Fixer replied to him by gargling. "He has already spilt milk on himself," said the small woman.

The Prime Minister held up her hand. Everyone stopped talking. "This is the best fixer I've met in my life," she said. "He's come from miles away to help us."

The Prime Minister cleaned the Fixer up and gave him his hat back. "Please, Mr Fixer," she said, smiling. "Would you fix the Sun so it rises again?"

The Fixer gargled with pride. Then he bounded around the room. The Fixer tripped up and fell into his ship. Then he was off into the dark sky.

After a short ride, the Fixer found the big, black Sun. He looked in his pile of tools and found it – the starspiker. He peeled away part of the Sun.

The Fixer jumped inside the Sun. It was full of big wires and bright lines. It looked like a very tricky job. The Fixer took off his hat. It was time to work.

The Fixer worked quickly. He wiped his face while he swapped fiddly pieces around. Soon he had put together all the parts perfectly, not a thing out of place.

The Sun was shining brightly again. The Fixer crash-landed back on Earth to see the Prime Minister. "Thank you so much," she said. "It is time for your payment."

"What would an alien like him want?" whispered the small woman.
"Is it gold? Silver? A new ship?" whispered the hairy man.

The Prime Minister walked to a big safe. She slowly opened the heavy door and pulled out... A sock.

The Fixer gargled as a way of thanking her.
Then he flew off in his ship.
"What a strange alien," said the wide man.
"Why would he want a sock?"

Far away in space, the Fixer bumped into his home. He stumbled through the front hole and took off his hat. Then the tired Fixer headed upstairs.

The children jumped up and down when they saw him. He smiled and pulled out the sock. The children gargled happily. Socks were the best toys. Every alien knew that.

The Fixer

1. How do you think the Prime Minister felt when she was woken up?

2. Why did the people on Earth need the Fixer's help?

3. What did the Fixer have for breakfast?
   (a) A smelly smoothie
   (b) Slime and goo pie
   (c) Fish soup

4. What did the Prime Minster give the Fixer for payment?

5. The people on Earth didn't believe the Fixer could help them. Why do you think that is? Would you have trusted the Fixer?

©2020 **BookLife Publishing Ltd.**
King's Lynn, Norfolk PE30 4LS

ISBN 978-1-83927-314-8

All rights reserved. Printed in Malaysia.
A catalogue record for this book is available from the British Library.

The Fixer
Written by John Wood
Illustrated by Amy Li

An Introduction to BookLife Readers...

Our Readers have been specifically created in line with the London Institute of Education's approach to book banding and are phonetically decodable and ordered to support each phase of the Letters and Sounds document.

Each book has been created to provide the best possible reading and learning experience. Our aim is to share our love of books with children, providing both emerging readers and prolific page-turners with beautiful books that are guaranteed to provoke interest and learning, regardless of ability.

BOOK BAND GRADED using the Institute of Education's approach to levelling.

PHONETICALLY DECODABLE supporting each phase of Letters and Sounds.

EXERCISES AND QUESTIONS to offer reinforcement and to ascertain comprehension.

BEAUTIFULLY ILLUSTRATED to inspire and provoke engagement, providing a variety of styles for the reader to enjoy whilst reading through the series.

**AUTHOR INSIGHT:
JOHN WOOD**

An incredibly creative and talented author, John Wood has written about 60 books for BookLife Publishing. Born in Warwickshire, he graduated with a BA in English Literature and English Language from De Montford University. During his studies, he learned about literature, styles of language, linguistic relativism, and psycholinguistics, which is the study of the effects of language on the brain. Thanks to his learnings, John successfully uses words that captivate and resonate with children and that will be sure to make them retain information. His stories are entertaining, memorable, and extremely fun to read.

This book is a 'b' level and is a purple level 8 book band.

She is fed up.
She wants to play too!

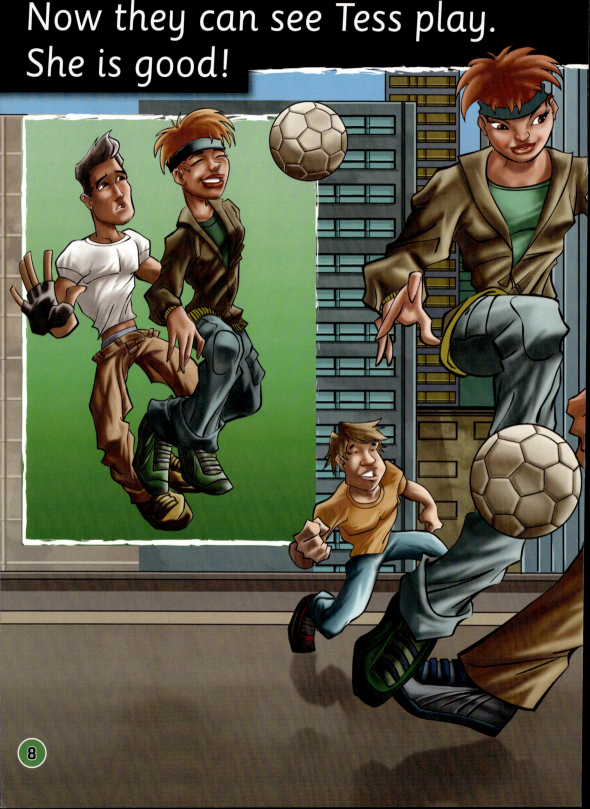

Now Tess is tops!

At the top — winning

At the top the fans yell for the team to win! It is mad but fun!

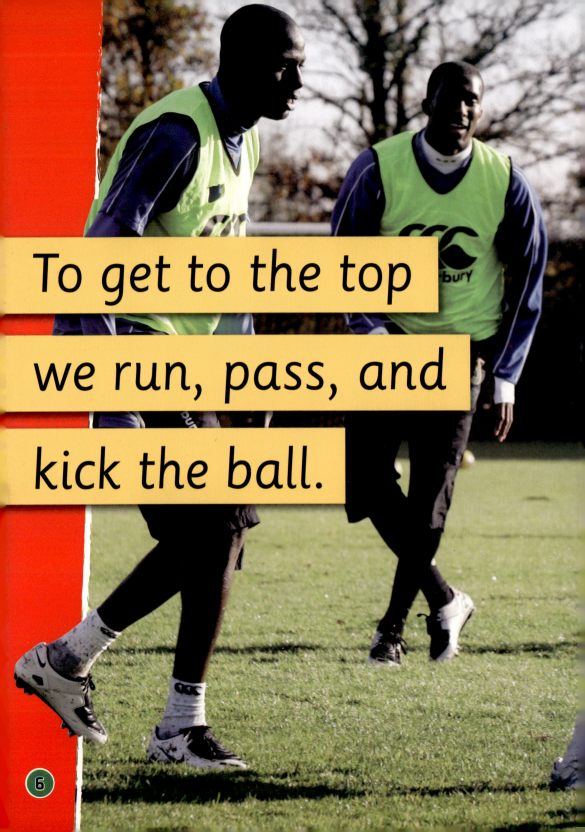

To get to the top we run, pass, and kick the ball.

Bit by bit we get skills to win.

Goal! At the top we cannot miss!

It is fun!

Oh yes ...

... it can be fun at the top!

You are the ref.

It is a toss up.

Refs are fit!

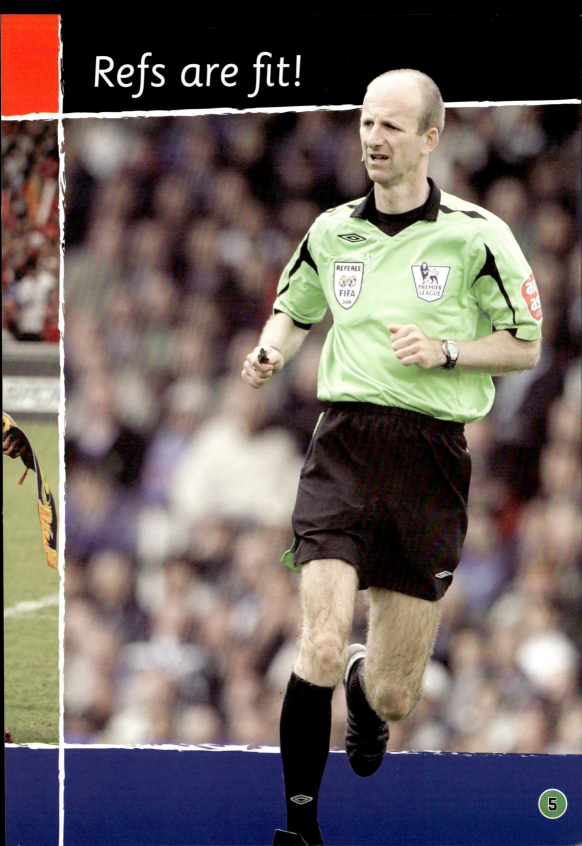

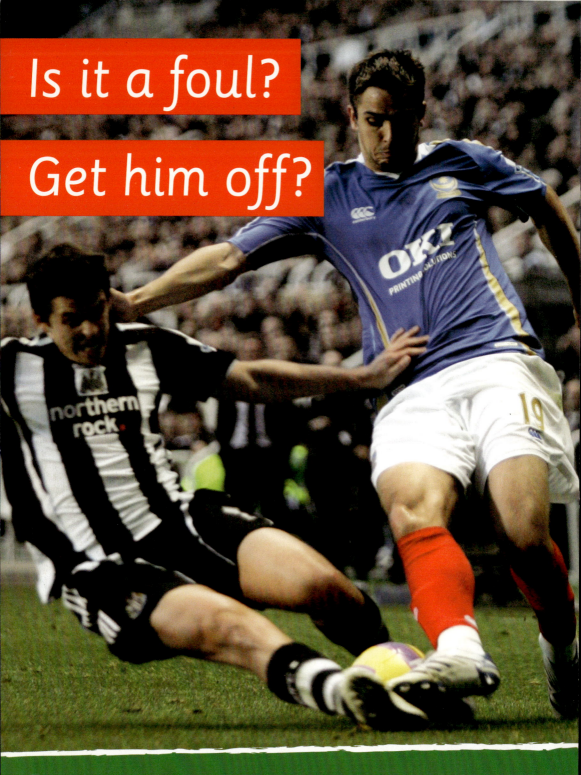

Is it a **red** ... or not?

Is the ball in the net?

It's up to you.
You are the ref!

Fans can boo the ref ...

... but refs do a top job.

Did you?